PRAISE FOR THE WORK
OF DAVID DEIDA

"David Deida must have the biggest balls in contemporary spirituality."

— Vijay Rana, *The Watkins Review*

"As a woman, I've never felt so understood and validated."

—Marci Shimoff, Co-Author of
Chicken Soup for the Woman's Soul

"The openness, the love! What lively new language David Deida finds for the unsayable!"

—Coleman Barks, Author of *The Essential Rumi*

"Every once in a while, someone comes along whose work is clearly a *next step*. Their ideas seem to answer some collective question hanging out in the culture. Their books and seminars become an underground buzz, and within a period of time, their ideas become part of our cultural vernacular. David Deida is such a person. In a time not too far off from now, his ideas will have spread like wildfire."

—Marianne Williamson, Author of *A Return to Love*

D1444702

"There are few categories I know of for an original like David Deida; for his teachings there is no pigeonhole. He is a bridge-builder between East and West, between ancient and modern wisdom traditions. David is in the dynamic living oral tradition of maverick spiritual teachers who, like free-jazz musicians, can riff directly on Reality, outside of established forms. Mark my words: in a future that I hope is not too far off, David Deida's original western Dharma will be widely known as one of the most sublime and accessible expressions of the essence of spiritual practice that is freely offered today."

—Lama Surya Das, Author of *Awakening the Buddha Within*

"David Deida's teachings on this central human concern, sexuality, emanate from a deeply trustworthy source. He has undergone his own rigorous training and practice, which manifests in precise, gentle, and thorough teachings. Like Zen, the fruition of David's work is openness, compassion, and love."

—Genpo Roshi, Author of *The Eye Never Sleeps*

"David Deida's work reveals a depth of loving the human condition and understanding its immanent spirituality I've seldom seen, even in a glimmer. It's hard for me to find words with which to express my appreciation and admiration for this unique gift."

—Jenny Wade, Ph.D., Author of *Changes of Mind*

INSTANT
ENLIGHTENMENT

Release
the Day
Therapeutic Massage

Rosa Casas,
NCTMB

**96 Roosevelt Street
St. Charles IL 60174**

630-234-5855

ALSO BY DAVID DEIDA

BOOKS

The Way of the Superior Man
*A Spiritual Guide to Mastering the
Challenges of Women, Work, and
Sexual Desire*

Dear Lover
*A Woman's Guide to Men, Sex, and
Love's Deepest Bliss*

Blue Truth
*A Spiritual Guide to Life & Death and
Love & Sex*

Intimate Communion
Awakening Your Sexual Essence

Finding God Through Sex
*Awakening the One of Spirit Through
the Two of Flesh*

Wild Nights
*Conversations with Mykonos about
Passionate Love, Extraordinary Sex,
and How to Open to God*

The Enlightened Sex Manual
Sexual Skills for the Superior Lover

It's a Guy Thing
An Owner's Manual for Women

AUDIO

Enlightened Sex
*Finding Freedom & Fullness through
Sexual Union*

**The Teaching Sessions:
The Way of the Superior Man**
*Revolutionary Tools and Essential Exercises
for Mastering the Challenges of Women,
Work, and Sexual Desire*

WEBSITE

deida.info

DAVID DEIDA

INSTANT
ENLIGHTENMENT
FAST, DEEP, AND SEXY

SOUNDS TRUE
awakening wisdom

Sounds True, Inc.
Boulder CO 80306

© 2007 by David Deida

SOUNDS TRUE is a trademark of Sounds True, Inc.

Cover and book design: Chad Morgan

First edition 2007
Printed in Canada

Library of Congress Cataloging-in-Publication Data

Deida, David.
  Instant enlightenment : fast, deep, and sexy / David Deida.
    p. cm.
  ISBN-13: 978-1-59179-560-5 (softcover)
  ISBN-10: 1-59179-560-5 (softcover)
  1. Spirituality. 2. Interpersonal relations. 3. Self-actualization
(Psychology). I. Title.

BL624.D3873 2007
170'.44--dc22

2006027361

✪ This book is printed on recycled paper containing
100% post-consumer waste and processed without chlorine.

10 9 8 7 6 5 4

CONTENTS

INTRODUCTION

If you want true happiness, here it is.

Enlightenment is free. It is love. It is openness.

And it is now, just as you are. This book will prove it to you, and show you how.

Enlightenment is *always* instant and sudden.

And usually forgotten, just as suddenly.

So repeat these brief exercises, which are often fast, endlessly deep, and sometimes downright sexy.

With humor, do them again and again, until you know that you are love. You are free. And you can't do anything less than give it away.

For the rest of your life, relax open this instant—while touching, eating, talking, and right now.

In short moments repeated often, unceasingly feel the openness of love that you are. In this way, you live as a gift to everyone.

Enlightenment is instant, but its expression evolves and deepens endlessly.

Pick a chapter, any chapter, and begin now.

●

GOD

What does it mean to open to God, or to love God?

Imagine somebody you love the most in your life, perhaps your child, your mother, your lover, or your best friend. Feel what it is to love that person.

Now, pick an object near you, like this book, or the floor beneath you, or a nearby pillow. Love whatever object you choose with the same intensity with which you love your most-loved person.

You may feel strange loving a book, floor, or pillow so fully, but you can do it. Practice loving until you feel your chosen object with the same love you offer your most-loved person.

When you can love an object as fully as your most-loved person, then practice loving the space around you. Love the space extending in front of you, behind you, left and right of you, above and below you. Love outwardly in all directions, with the same feeling with which you open to your most-loved person.

Then practice loving everything within you—even your darkest secret places of shame and perversity—with the same love you offer to your most-loved person. This may take some time, or you may be able to do it right away.

If you love one person, you can love God. God is everything and what is beyond everything—all of which you can love. Love everything and everyone whom you know and don't know, and you are loving God. Open to everything inside and outside of you, even the unknowable mystery beyond everything. Open to feel and love all, the visible and the unknown. This is opening to God, or loving God.

Every instant you love so fully is enlightenment. But because you are habitually used to contracting your feelings, in the next instant you may suddenly find yourself absorbed in picking your nose or scratching your chin as you work for world peace by writing your congressman.

Your loving may be truncated for days as you become lost in duties, chores, and emotions—raising a family, succeeding at a career, talking, sexing, or eating. You may not be opening to God for the sake of your temporary experience. Your ever-changing life never quite fulfills you for good, and you know it.

Instant enlightenment is to love, right now, as if you were loving your most-loved person. No matter what you are feeling or experiencing, inwardly or outwardly, you can love without holding anything back. This is what it means to love God.

So start by feeling the person you love the most, and open to include every aspect of each moment in the openness of your love.

Offering yourself open in this way is instant enlightenment.

Forgetting to love is the usual life of subtle torment.

SHOP

Feel all the garments in your favorite clothing store. Imbibe the many colors. Let your fingertips graze the textures of dobby, satin, and fur. Try on whatever you like. Bask in wearing first one glorious outfit, then another.

Continue to do this, while feeling all the people in the world who are at war, diseased, or in lonely despair— while you enjoy your shopping trip. Start close to home, with your family and friends, knowing their private suffering or secret pain.

Then, expand to feel everyone on earth who may be starving, sick, or dying. From your heart, radiate to them the happiness of trying on such beautiful clothing. Offer them the feeling of the fabrics and the color of the clothing as gifts. Imagine beaming your wonderful experience of shopping to all those who are suffering.

To be free as love, give your joy away.

Give all your wonderful experiences away to others, as gifts, keeping nothing, not even a memory, for yourself. Guilt and tension result from hoarding your happy moments. Instant enlightenment is to give all your happiness away to others.

ORAL

Everything feels enlarged in your mouth. A small sore or a tiny grain of sand can seem huge. Your lips and tongue are exquisitely sensitive to giving and receiving pleasure, tasting both the delicious and the bitter.

A jellyfish has no tongue. Perhaps its whole body is as sensitive as your tongue is. Pretend that your whole body is tongue-sensitive. Imagine licking your socks, tasting the inside of your pants, French-kissing the book you are holding.

Perhaps luckily, your whole body isn't like this. Your taste organ is sheltered from bombarding flavors. Your tongue is protected in your mouth, behind teeth and bony jaws.

A tree has no tongue, and will never taste the salty sweat of a trembling lover. Yet a tree dances its leaves in the sunshine and rain, rooting down and dirty in the rich, damp earth, without stress of career or thoughts of death. A tree has no tongue, but in its own way, it is singing from its roots to its leaves, "I'm alive!"

Next time you use your mouth sexually, be grateful that you can. Allow the experience of oral sex to expand and fill your awareness. Explore the landscape of oral sensations, the tastes and textures you lick and nibble and suck. Get lost in oral sex, as only a human does.

Before this birth and after death, you probably have no tongue. Who knows? But right now, in your human form, what is the most artful way to give joy with your mouth? How can you offer your soft tongue and skilled lips as a gift for the sake of others?

You can certainly give your lover pleasure by stimulating his or her neck, earlobes, nipples, thighs, feet, or genitals with your tongue and lips. But can you offer your mouth for this purpose: to enable your lover to offer ever-present openness as unfettered love for the sake of all beings?

This is the enlightened purpose of sex. Oral sex is unique, because our mouths are so sensitive. Proportionately, more of your brain's capacity is dedicated to your tongue and lips than to any other body part. Obviously, a drop of salty water causes a different reaction if dripped on your back than on your tongue. So much more so for a genital's texture and flavor between your lips. Your mouth knows the most of what it touches.

Try tiny little licks or nibbles,
movements smaller than a grain
of sand. Allow your lover to feel
just how sensitive your mouth is by
the groans and ahs that sound out
as your tongue and lips discover
explosive flavors and extreme
textures of curve and ruffle that no
redwood will ever feel. Let your dog
in the next room wonder why you
are moaning so.

Turn your tasted flavors into sounds,
which allows your lover to feel your
amplified responsiveness, connecting
your hearts, enlarging love to
flow between your two bodies.
This is the point: to convert your
mouth's extreme sensitivity into the
magnification of love.

Lip-lapping love relaxes the boundaries between selves. Orally enlarged love lingers long after your tonguing has ceased and your sucking has stopped.

This love's afterglow your pet can feel; so can a redwood, believe it or not, and certainly your children and friends can feel your tenderized and vulnerable heart all day. Your liberated love is a blessing in their lives.

Enlarged love offered to others
is what your tongue can sexually
expose. Why not? Anything less
would be an under-use of your
human form. Trees have their own
blessing style. Offer your most
sensitive human part as a gift,
tendering love-swelled blessings to all.

MOVIE

What is one of your favorite movies?

Remember what you liked about this great movie, its action, romance, or characters.

Now, suppose you are watching this movie on video. You have a special fast-forwarding control device.
You can speed the movie up just a little so it's difficult to follow what's happening, or make it go really fast so it's just a blur.

Starting from normal speed, how fast can you speed it up and still find the movie interesting? Eventually, the image is moving so fast that you lose interest. At what point does the story no longer hold your attention due to its speed?

You can also imagine slowing down the movie. A tiny bit slower is fine. The voices are a little lower and people are moving like molasses, but you can still follow the plot. However, if you go slower and slower—until it requires three minutes for an actor to take one step—the movie becomes intolerable to watch. It's too boring; not enough is happening.

You are only interested in stories that move at a certain speed. You can actually determine your personal range for this speed-of-interest by doing the experiment just described with your favorite movie. You may find that your friends can enjoy the movie after you lose interest because the movie is going too fast or too slow for you but is still okay for them. Your speed-of-interest is personal.

Obviously, much is happening in the world around you that is too fast or too slow to interest you. Grass grows too slowly to interest you. High-frequency sound waves move too fast but still catch your dog's attention.

What you actually think of as your world—the drama you pay attention to, your real-life story, your work and love life—is composed of happenings moving at a certain speed.

If you could see your whole life played in fast speed so its entire duration lasted one minute, the blur of images and feelings wouldn't interest you. Your life would be moving too fast to notice the everyday dramas. Your attention wouldn't get wrapped up in the one-minute flash. Likewise, if your life were slowed down so that it took years to walk across a room, you'd go crazy with boredom.

Nevertheless, parts of your life *are* happening really fast—such as the constant motion of your eyeballs. Scientists call it *physiological nystagmus,* a high-frequency tremor of the eye that serves to continuously shift the image on the retina.

Your hair, on the other hand, grows far too *slowly* to occupy your attention. You only notice when it's finally grown too long.

Yet, the angry argument with your spouse about who forgot to pay the utility bill *does* occupy your concern. The quarrel happens at a precise speed, which catches your attention more than your hair as it lengthens or your eyes as they oscillate.

Everything happening too fast or slow to catch your attention goes unnoticed. The human domain of drama has a very narrow range, indeed; yet we take it very seriously.

Instant enlightenment is to feel the rigid and arbitrary timescale of your life's drama. You are concerned about the tiny part of your life-in-motion that occurs between too fast and too slow. From a geological timescale, your life pops faster than a corn kernel in hot oil. It's done in an instant. Yet, from your human perspective, daily events seem massively significant.

You can actually train yourself to experience events moving faster and slower, expanding the range of the story you can follow and understand. This has a profound effect on your capacity to offer love to others, rather than get caught up in popcorn moments.

Sit still and learn to feel the formation of a single thought, as if watching a balloon being slowly inflated, before it pops to gone.

Closely follow the building-up drama of one thought, applying the same interest with which you engage a typical conversation.

When the story of each of your billions of daily thoughts is as interesting—or as boring—as the drama of a normal conversation, then your anxious sense of self-concern will begin to loosen.

As your tension loosens, so does your speed-range, and soon humor softens the tightness of dread, hope, and fear as your life story plays out.

As you loosen to embrace the whole scale of time, then the humor of being so tightly engaged in the itsy-bitsy movie of the narrow human speed widens you further.

Nothing is lost in this spaciousness.
Your birth, life, and death remain
vividly felt; your heart is still torn by
your lover's betrayal. Your spirits
are lifted by the scent of a rose
or a baby's sudden smile. All is
embraced, including what's usually
too fast and too slow for the common
human speed of life. And your
humor opens as vast as existence.

When you can do this exercise—
really feel the speed-range of your
attention and care, not just think
about it intellectually—then your
love is freed from time.

Freely fast: You can intuitively feel the exquisitely crystallizing, sudden, blurring-to-invisibility speed of prior light taking form as your lover's shapely appearance, noticed only after the fact, like this entire moment, which actually occurred nanoseconds ago, before being processed by your eye and brain into a perceivable image you call "now."

Freely slow: You can relax as the waiting-forever of continental drift, as oceans form and islands erupt from volcanic upheavals.

You still may prefer watching life's
movies at normal human speed:
your child playing with a kitten, your
lover remembering your birthday.
But on either side of each moment's
speed, massive dramas are unfolding,
involving countless beings, large and
small, within which your life's drama
is but an evanescent pop.

Anytime you notice that life is
getting you down, you can imagine
fast-forwarding your life's movie
until it becomes a blur. Then, find
out where your attention goes
when the images of your lifespan
no longer hold you, and your love
widens suddenly to light.

●

MANGLE

Imagine you are mangled in a car accident. Metal has sliced through your body. You are lying on the pavement in a puddle of blood.

Imagine sleeping in a soft bed, or being mangled in a car accident. The difference you feel is made from the same thoughts that create your personal suffering. What does this mean? How do you discover the cause of your suffering and the source of true happiness? What does any of this have to do with car accidents and beds? Try this experiment to get the answers.

Go between these two feelings, back and forth: Relaxed, lying in a big, comfy bed. Mangled, lying in a puddle of blood. Picture each, feel both, one and then the other. Again and again. Brightly see and acutely feel the images. Mangled body. Soft bed.

Now, instantly, feel the "who" that *can* feel both pictures, and relax as that "who" now.

You are this capacity to feel.

(The images were just targets for your attention. The true you is the feeling-openness that notices the movement of attention between the images.)

You are the space where the pictures happen, where attention moves between a mangled body and a soft bed. The imagery changes but the feeling-openness—who you are—is always unchangingly open to feel.

Instant enlightenment is to relax open as this capacity to feel, whatever picture is happening now. Then you are free to feel, regardless of what is happening, and you can act as love.

If you forget this openness of feeling even for a fraction of a second, then you seem trapped again. Remember this openness that you are, and you will instantly find out that love acts spontaneously, untrapped by the present picture of your life.

Don't believe a word of this. Discover what is true for yourself when you do this exercise. See if you change with the picture, or if you are the openness where the picture happens, the openness who feels the changes.

Test enlightenment now. Mangled body. Soft bed. The images have changed.

In what space does the light of your imagination shine?

Is this feeling-openness who you are any different than ever?

●

BUG

You are in a grassy park. You are a bug that has crawled beneath a pile of dog poop. You are nestled between the park lawn and the warm mound of feces. It is dark and stinky, but safe. You can eat the crap around you. You don't have to do anything but eat, breathe, and excrete while relaxing in the grass beneath the pile.

Look around where you are right now. Why do you prefer being here over living as a bug beneath dog crap? What feels good in your current environment? Clean surfaces? Fresh air? Potential sexual partners and friends who are shaped like you?

Your desire for these specific qualities—and more—has resulted in you appearing as a human to yourself. During dreams, you may have experienced what it feels like to appear as a non-human.

Whether appearing as a happy human in your home or a dung bug in your dreams, are you willing to give love now? Or, are you waiting to love until your life gets better?

When your life seems crappy, you always have a choice: you can wait and depress your love, or you can give your gift of love right now.

No matter where you find yourself, in heaven or hell, you can make this commitment: I am appearing here to offer love to everyone also appearing here, and I will do so as best as I can.

This can be your vow: I offer myself to be *lived by love*, as a gift for the sake of others.

No matter where you find yourself lodged, you can be alive as love's offering. Love is a force that is larger than you. Love lives *through* you.

When love can't find a way to live through you, then your psyche suffers and depression may haunt you.

Even while depressed, love breaks through your sense of futility in little bursts: in your child's laughter, the smell of coffee, or the light of sunrise. Love breaks through your despair and you are grateful to be alive, for just a moment.

Practice this gratefulness, even while wanting to die. Offer yourself to be lived by love, especially when your life seems crappy.

Enlightenment is the capacity to open and be lived by the love that is already, miraculously, living your life, despite all your current torment and refusal. Instant enlightenment is to offer love now—whatever the circumstance—without waiting for things to get better.

Things will get better, but they will also get worse. You can count on that, so why not open and be lived by love as an offering now?

Allow love to breathe you, with every inhalation and exhalation. Allow love to move your body and soul. Even if you find yourself born as a bug living under poop, allow your entire life to be animated by love's force, and you are as free as you can be.

●

HATE

Hate everyone you see today. Hate strangers, family, and friends. Look at each person and generate feelings of hate.

Don't slack off. If you aren't hating, then work at it. Hate the woman in the car in front of you. Hate the man you last spoke with on the phone. Hate the next person you see, intensely.

As you hate, imagine yourself dying, right now, while hating. Hate, and feel as if you are dying. Would you rather die a different way than hating?

How would you rather die?

Live the answer to this question—
offer the disposition in which you
wish to die—from now on.

If you notice yourself slacking off,
then, once again, practice hating
every person you come upon. Really
hate him or her, hating as hard as
you can, and feel if this is how you
want to die, in hate.

Relax open to be lived by the force
of love. If this feels difficult, then hate
for just an instant to help you commit
to how *loving* you want to be when
you die, which could be right now.

PRAISE

Imagine praising the next person you see. Praise him or her as fully as possible, so you are embarrassed that you are so praiseful. What praise would you give? Picture someone you know—anyone—and feel what is the most magnanimous praise you can offer them.

Remember your mother and father as you offer this praise. Imagine doing so now. How do you feel?

You have probably chosen a career and sought an intimate partner in reaction to the praise you never got from your parents. Take time to remember what you didn't get from your mother and father, and look at what you seek through your career and intimate relationship.

What do you wish your parents had told you more? Really feel into your childhood. Feel, as a child, what your parents said or didn't say to you. What do you wish your parents had given you more of? What do you wish your parents had said to you?

To the next person you see, silently give the praise you didn't get enough of from your parents but wish you had. Give this praise silently to everyone you see for the next three days. In your imagination, give this praise silently to your parents, right now. How does it feel to offer the praise you never got, but wished you had?

Holding back praise limits all the love you are willing to give—through speech, sex, and touch. It also restrains the love you could offer through your life's work.

Give the praise that you wish your parents had given you more of. Give it silently to everyone, and give it out loud to your lover, whether you feel they deserve it or not. Find out what happens when you do. Discover the full offering you were born to give, as a gift, to everyone.

●

MASTURBATE

As you read these words right now, feel what you are most afraid you might read under the heading "Masturbate." Quickly, right now, what are you afraid you might read? (Think about it before you proceed to the next paragraph.)

"Masturbate" is the title of the chapter. Once you can feel what you were afraid you might read, then imagine yourself doing it. Whatever you were afraid you might read under the heading "Masturbate," imagine yourself doing it in a way that your body relaxes and your heart opens so you can offer your love to others more fully.

Imagine all the people in the world are watching you, and pleasure yourself for them—so their hearts open.

Your life feels smaller than you know it could be. Why? Part of the reason is your fear of unashamed pleasure. This fear curtails the whole-bodied flow of life's force that you can enjoy even all by yourself.

If you want pleasure, there are no excuses and nobody else to blame. Either you have no limits whatsoever to the pleasure you allow to flow through your body, or you are harboring fear. Pleasure is energy. And energy is the movement of love. Is love free to move through every part of your body while masturbating?

If you didn't even bother to feel what you are most afraid of reading under the chapter title "Masturbate," then you are probably too hesitant or doubtful to accomplish much of importance in your life. You'll feel that true love or inspiration is lacking, or that you just don't have the energy.

Imagine masturbating to God-given ecstasy. Open your heart and offer your body to love's force, exploding like silken electricity through your trembling, vibrant flesh, regardless of your fear, shame, or laziness.

If you can't, or if you won't, then you are chronically under-offering your body as a source of love's energy. To offer yourself fully, relax your whole body as love's pleasure, and imagine radiating happiness to everyone.

First, open *yourself* to love's flow, regardless of your fear. Then, you will be able to open others to love's radiant pleasure.

●

SWEAR

What is the dirtiest word you know?
Whatever word is the filthiest for you,
say it out loud when you are alone.

Say it several times. Then say, "I love
you," imagining that you are with
someone you love. Say, "I love you,"
several times, with real feeling.

Alternate between saying your
dirtiest word and "I love you," until
you can say the dirty word with as
much love, heart openness, and soft
benediction as "I love you."

Then, with a trusted friend or lover, alternate saying your chosen bad word and "I love you" out loud, until he or she feels your love equally transmitted through both expressions.

Choose another filthy word, and repeat this process. Bad word, I love you, bad word, I love you ... until the felt offering of your love is carried equally by both expressions.

After turning bad words into carriers of your love, practice saying *every* word that you utter, from now until you die, in a way that feels like "I love you" to whoever hears it.

When you notice yourself speaking lovelessly, return to this exercise, starting with the filthiest word you can think of, until you can speak every word, once again, as a felt carrier of love. This may take minutes, or decades, of practice.

●

TUSSLE

Imagine you have a lover whom you trust. Look into his or her eyes until you feel each other's love fully, as if your hearts were entirely connected. With your *right* hand, sensually caress your lover, as your lover caresses you. When you feel your lover's love lessening—perhaps he or she becomes distracted or self-absorbed—lift your *left* hand as a signal.

When you feel love diminish in your lover's gaze-from-the-heart, raise your left hand. At this signal, you and your lover remove physical contact until full love-connection is reestablished through your mutual gaze. Then, when undiminished love is once again felt by both of you, lower your hand and continue caressing.

Of course, your lover may also raise his or her hand when the love-connection between you is felt to diminish. Both of you remain true to your agreement *to stop caressing and remove physical contact* until love comes back to felt-fullness through your deep heart-gazing. Only then should touch be reengaged.

When you get good at sensually caressing each other, maintaining a gaze of full love, and feeling connected heart to heart, then you are ready for the next step.

Start by adding dirty words. If saying dirty words causes the felt love-connection to diminish, then your or your lover's left hand should be raised, and talking and touching should stop. When love is reestablished—when you both can feel your hearts connected and your gaze is deep into each other's open soul—then continue touching and talking dirty.

Practice this until you can say anything, even swear at each other, and still maintain deep heart-connection and humor.

When you can do this, add a further step: practice tussling. Perhaps you start by pinching each other, tickling, or wrestling. Maintain deep heart-gazing even while tussling. Each of you can raise your hand anytime you feel love diminish, whereupon you stop all actions and remove physical contact.

Resume tussling when, through gazing into each other's soul, you both trust what you feel.

In real life, you can raise your left hand with your lover at any time to indicate that it's time to connect deeper, even in the middle of heated arguments or when one of you genuinely feels hurt. By doing so, you can learn to instantly reestablish a deep heart-to-heart connection with your lover simply through gazing, opening, and feeling each other's love.

Start by playing with sensual caressing, swearing, and tussling, while giving feedback by raising your hand and gazing into your lover's eyes when feeling a disconnection between your hearts. Through this process, you will learn to reconnect with your lover even in the course of a sudden and real altercation—the kind that might usually take hours, or even days, to resolve.

The way of instant loving can really be this fast, deep, and sexy, if you are willing to feel through your emotional resistances as well as your lover's, and to allow your otherwise recoiling hearts to connect and relax together in trust.

●

COVET

Think of something you covet. A
new pair of shoes. Your friend's
Mercedes-Benz. A perfect lover. Five
million dollars. What comes to your
mind first, something you really
want but don't have?

Now, imagine that you did have it.
How would you act, right now? How
would you feel, right now?

Act and feel as if you had what you coveted, right now. Breathe, move, blink, and enact the facial expression as if you had it. Act this way for a few minutes, feeling abundant with what you really covet.

Is acting and feeling this way fundamentally better than how you were acting and feeling before you imagined abundance?

If the answer is yes, then continue acting and feeling this way. Why not allow yourself to feel abundance now? Why wait for an external excuse?

If the answer is that feeling this way is not fundamentally better, then ignore your coveting, because getting what you want won't make you feel or act any better than now.

Here is the easy way to say it:

1. Act like you would feel if you had everything you wanted. Or,

2. Ignore your desires because they don't lead to happiness in any case.

Either way, you are free.

●

KILL

Pretend you are going to kill the next person you see. Feel this in your body, emotions, and thoughts. Imagine that you are really going to kill this person. How do you feel inside?

Now, imagine that you are going to have sex with the next person you see, male or female. Again, how do you feel inside?

One last exercise: Pretend you are going to save the life of the next person you see. But in doing so, your own life will end. Imagine you are going to die while saving this person's life. How do you feel inside?

Which imagined action—killing, sexing, or saving while dying—most feels like liberation, freedom, and unbound love?

Why would you intentionally hold anything in your mind, except that which most opens your heart and soul so that others may benefit from your openness?

From now on, the choice is yours. When you find yourself imagining something that results in you feeling less open, simply imagine whatever most opens you.

This is the first step, to replace habits of closure with habits of openness. The next step is to hang loose as awareness in space, sustaining openness without support, *being* openness without effort or intention.

After you intentionally imagine whatever most opens you—perhaps saving your best friend's life—allow this image or feeling to dissolve in openness, like a swirl dissolving in water. Let go of all effort to imagine anything, not adulterating love's open water.

In another moment, you may find yourself once again thinking of something—perhaps a person you dislike—that closes you, even a little bit. What can you do?

First, intentionally visualize or feel whatever most opens your heart, softens your belly, and relaxes your mind—for instance, making passionate love with an enlightened lover as if your bodies were emanations of bliss-light.

Then, allow this visualization to dissolve in uncontrived feeling, like swirling water uncurling in an ocean of love's openness, alive as the bright space of now.

Replace unloving mind-forms with loving ones. Then, allow all forms to relax open as love's clear gush of light. Repeat this two-step process whenever you happen to notice that you are closing, so openness prevails in every moment that you naturally remember. This is the practice of instant love-openness, no matter what else you are doing in your life.

NIPPLES

Squeeze your own nipples until they almost hurt but are still tingling with pleasure. You can actually do this, or simply imagine it, or have your trusted lover pinch your nipples so hard they are on the verge of hurting but you are still mostly feeling pleasure.

Repeat this until you can simply *remember* the feeling of almost-painful pleasure in your nipples whenever you want.

The next time you feel bothered
by anything at all, remember this
sensation of almost-painful pleasure
in your nipples.

Offer this feeling in your nipples
to your ancestors, in gratitude for
the suffering they experienced so
you could be born and have your
nipples squeezed to pleasure. It's
such a small offering for what they
endured so you could be living now.
It's probably also more bodily-felt
gratitude than you typically offer in
any random moment.

Offer this feeling in your nipples
to everyone who has ever hurt
you in any way, in gratitude for
the opportunity to learn to give the
pleasure from your nipples instead of
the pain from your memory.

Imagine that you were a great spiritual being, perhaps Jesus of Nazareth, or the Buddha from India, or Yeshe Tsogyal of Tibet, or Mother Teresa from Albania. Also imagine that your whole body is as sensitive as your nipples.

Imagine yourself to be your chosen holy man or woman. Radiate pleasure on the verge of pain from your whole body—pleasure so intense it is almost too much to bear. Imagine radiating this pleasure to all other beings.

What expression do you have on your face as your whole nipple-like body offers the unbearable pleasure-pain of being?

Why have you chosen not to show this expression more often, for real, while offering love so openly it hurts?

Great spiritual beings love so much it hurts. You can, too. Start with your nipples.

●

WEAR

Pretend you are wearing the body of someone else. Choose a person nearby—your friend on the couch next to you, or the stranger in front of you in a checkout line at the grocery store—and inhabit his or her body.

Wear this person's facial expression, jaw position, and forehead wrinkles. Wear his or her hands' gestures, chest's elasticity, or breast's weight. Adopt his or her neck's angularity and feet's positioning.

In detail, feel what it would be to live *as* this body, with the same genitals, the same accumulation of tensions, the same history-etched flesh of betrayal and regret. Breathe as this body is breathing. Intuitively, feel its aches and tingles.

While wearing this other person's body, relax as it. Just like you might put on your old favorite coat and then relax inside, put on this person's body and relax. Allow yourself to open and feel what you imagine this person is feeling on the inside—darkness or brightness, sadness or glee—and relax as these feelings.

Next, relax and open while feeling yourself wearing the body of as many people as you can, feeling their stance, stride, sensations, and moods. Eventually, feel flowers and mountains and even chairs: wear their shape, relax as their form, and open as love's offering, just as they are. How would it feel to be a telephone, or your postal delivery person, and to open as love's offering *as that form*?

The truth is, you *are* everything that appears in your experience. At the depth of feeling-openness, there is no other, no separation from anything or anyone, even though their forms *seem* separate and distinct on the surface of appearances.

Fear is pulling back to feel as if you were inside of something separate from open space. If you don't add fear, then quite naturally you wear everyone and the whole appearing world as your body, feeling everything without boundaries or borders.

Without holding back, wear everyone's mood and shape. Feel every kindness and horror. Breathing and feeling and being all, relax open as all. Be feeling-openness, with or without form. This is instant enlightenment and its practice.

●

INSIDE

Go inside yourself as deep as you can. Feel inward, deeper and deeper. Is there an end to how deeply you can feel? If not, keep feeling inwardly until you are certain inward never ends.

All there is inside is deeper and deeper openness.

Now, feel outwardly as far as you can. Listen to the most distant sounds you can hear, and then listen further, into the openness beyond the farthest sound.

Notice the most distant light, and then gaze beyond it, into the endless openness.

As if feeling your surroundings for ghosts, goose bumps tingling your skin open to the air, feel endlessly outward with your whole body as far as you can: feeling goes open, on and on.

Now, simultaneously, feel the openness that goes on and on, both inwardly *and* outwardly. Really do this, and you will discover that feeling never ends in any direction. The most basic sense of being, of existence, is the openness of feeling in all directions. Being is feeling wide open.

As soon as your feeling stops short of on-and-on, feel whatever you are feeling (a tree or a thought), and feel beyond it. You don't have to stop feeling anything (you can still feel the tree or the thought), but also feel the openness that goes beyond any thing. Feel further than you've ever felt before, zillions of miles inwardly and zillions of miles outwardly, on and on, wide open.

This is who you are, this wide openness, feeling with no boundaries.

Be openness, feeling on and on, while having sex or during a conversation, and your lover and friends will begin to feel as unbound openness, too.

Do you have a better way to live your life? The choice is yours.

●

JAW

Grind your jaw. Hunch your shoulders. Breathe shallowly. Tighten your gut.

Now imagine making love with your ideal lover.

As if making love, allow your body to open as it would with your lover, in full trust, lusciousness, and passionate communion. Allow your body to relax wide open as if in the most sacred and profound sexual embrace.

Sustain this feeling of communion, trust, and pleasure, as you once again grind your jaw while tensing your shoulders, breath, and belly.

In other words, feel like you are making the most beautiful love imaginable, even while your body squeezes shut. At first, this will be difficult, because tightening your body makes you feel bad inside. But after trying several times, you'll be able to imagine yourself making love in the arms of your beloved, even while your body is tight.

Right now, most folks in the world are, to some degree, tightening—just as you are in this exercise. But few people are loving as if they were having the best sex ever. Most people are tense, suffering, closing, and feeling a lack of love.

The next time you are with someone who seems like they are tense and suffering, assume (or "wear") *their* tension as *your* body, but *also* feel like you are making love.

Maybe you can even assume the tension of a whole room full of people, and simultaneously feel as if your heart were wide open in bright communion with your ideal lover.

Eventually, you don't have to physically enact the tension of others in your body, but just feel their actual suffering. Allow your body to relax open while you feel their suffering, your heart glowing as if making splendid love with your chosen lover.

As an exercise, then, breathe in the suffering of others. Breathe in their malaise and anxiety, and let their suffering dissolve in the glow of your heart's open love. Sometimes it helps to temporarily shape your body in the form of their tension. Wear their kinked form and then relax as love's effortless openness.

While breathing in and feeling the suffering of others, you may notice your jaw grinding or your belly tightening. Instantly remember the feeling of making love, and allow your heart's remembrance to relax your body while radiating openness out to others.

Enlightenment is feeling your own tension, as well as the misery of others, while still being willing and able to offer the deepest love you can give—as if the whole world were your lover who was hurting.

●

DOLLAR

Imagine going to a public place with a group of friends. Pick friends with whom you feel most safe.

With your group of friends, imagine locating a trustworthy-looking stranger whom you find sexy.

Imagine giving a dollar to this sexy stranger. Look him or her in the eyes and say, "I'm doing this as part of an assigned exercise. I'm supposed to give a dollar to somebody really sexy. Then I am to have no further contact with you."

As you imagine doing this exercise, how does it feel to give someone a dollar while saying he or she is sexy?

Most of us are complicated about both sex and money. These are forms of energy exchange, which can be as simple as an unexpected gift, or as complicated as a lawsuit.

Sex and money: the sources of most of our desire and disappointment, our hope and fear.

Enlightenment means to live every moment so that no residue remains but the openness of love.

Sex and money are often our least enlightened domains, the areas tainted with the most residues. Therefore, few people can imagine doing this exercise without a lingering "charge" of emotional complication.

Often, the best ways to discover the enlightened use of sex and money is to break the usual rules in the least risky ways, in order to find out where sexual obstructions and financial blocks reside within you.

Repeat this exercise, or do others that require you to imagine offering gifts beyond your comfort zone. As you learn to give lovingly despite your fears, your sexual and financial lives can be lived according to what truly serves openness the most, rather than being inhibited by your residual fear-gunk, holding your offering back.

You can become stuck in your own dramas of sex and money. What you can't live as openness, offered without residue, creates stickiness in your life. Yet the price of discovering your tar of unfinished business, your sexual and financial traumas and fears, may exceed what you are willing to wager.

Do you harbor no sexual or financial secrets?

These secrets are among your most hidden refusals to open as love.

Are you willing to face, feel, confess, and open beyond your every sexual and financial fear and complication now? Human birth is for those who are *not* quite ready but may be on the verge—that's why you are here as you are.

If your issue was about spawning eggs in gravel, you would have been born a fish.

●

DESPAIR

Life often hurts. Your children can become injured or diseased, or die. You can suffer financial loss or bankruptcy. The world's military forces often bomb innocent men and women, and terrorists can attack at any time, limbs and lives exploding apart forever.

While breast-feeding, sharing tea, or playing golf, your heart may simply stop pumping for genetically predetermined reasons.

We experience moments of great comfort and peace, but as we age, our bodies develop aches, we lose our friends and families, and our despair can easily grow.

Feel your despair now, however slight or devastating it may be. Most likely, you can find the place in you that is despairing due to some loss, some feeling of loneliness or futility.

While feeling this despair, notice that everything continues happening.

Your heart still beats, if you are alive.

Colors and shapes of light continue to shine; your environment continues to appear.

Your thoughts continue as you read
these words.

Stuff is happening, inwardly
and outwardly. Despair may be
happening, too.

Along with everything else, you are
happening. All that you can call
"you"—your inner sense of self,
your perceptions, your emotions
and thoughts, your memories—is
happening.

If you feel despair, feel it *happening*.
Its energy moves and feels a certain
way that you call "despair." Feel this
energy completely.

Relax with it. Instead of pulling away from its discomfort, relax into despair, willing to feel its pain.

Tenderly explore despair as if you were examining the most sensitive parts of a just-traumatized lover.

Notice if you resist feeling despair. Are you avoiding the ongoing wound of futility, suffering, and lonely sorrow that quivers beneath the surface of your daily life?

Relax your resistance so you can feel the trauma of despair fully. In your genitals, belly, heart, and throat, feel how your whole body has been torn by despair.

Where is the experience of your heart-wounded body?

Where are *you* happening?

While feeling the pain of despair,
also feel its living buoyancy,
quivering in feeling-space.

Despair—if you feel it fully, without
resistance—is quaking open like a
raw wound in space.

Just so, *everything* that happens is
experienced in a felt-space.

Sadness, betrayal, and joy happen
in emotional-space. Tickles, warmth,
and sharpness happen in touch-
space. Honking horns, tweeting
birds, and laughter happen in aural-
space. Your thoughts move in mind-
space. Every feeling is buoyantly
happening in an open feeling-space
with no edge.

All space is aware, or capable of feeling, and full of living energy: sounds, thoughts, colors, and emotions.

Despair is compatible with enlightenment because enlightenment is the living space of feeling-openness. Your experience, including despair, is rippling as this openness.

Love is another name for this feeling-openness, who you are, what everything ripples as, including despair.

Openness is the love that is living you right now—even though you may hurt tremendously.

Gratitude is the posture of acknowledging that love's feeling-openness is living you.

Be grateful, and you are free.

Maybe you have already died, and this is the afterworld. Or, perhaps you are asleep and dreaming this very moment. In any case, you are openness, so why resist any feeling?

Despair and gratitude occupy the same space of feeling, regardless of how long your current self and world last—lit up, open, and floating—in this feeling-space.

Risk loving everything, including despair, by feeling it fully, with gratitude. Find out how open now is. Love everything as it is, and you are free to act with the courage of love that spontaneously quivers as the infinite openness of every happening, including despair.

●

SLEEP

Where do you fall when you "fall" asleep?

Close your eyes, and fall there now. Literally, let go and *fall* inside, pretending to be deeply asleep. Feel this sleep-place of silent, blissful nothingness, right now.

Are you smiling? If not, close your eyes and fall into the dark peacefulness of this sleep-place until you can't help but smile in bliss.

When you have accomplished this capacity to feel the place you fall asleep to, then try this: dream.

Dreamily imagine yourself sitting in the wilderness, watching two elephants eating grass with their trunks, while a monkey shouts from the trees, "Hey, buddy, you're dreaming!"

Imagination is a form of daydreaming.

When you have examined your imaginative daydreaming, then open your eyes and see the world around you. Is it possible to know for sure that this isn't a dream, too?

Have you ever wakened from a dream only to discover that you are still dreaming? Most people have.

If this were a dream right now, would you act any differently?

Whether you are dreaming or awake, one thing is certain: It will end. You will wake up from the dream and it will evaporate.

Your life as you know it vanishes at death; your entire lifetime disappears, as if your turmoils, adventures, and romances had never occurred.

As you age, you may begin to feel the futility of your life, as if it were a fading dream. The routine cycles of days and nights can easily grind down your grand hopes for fulfillment as you slide into old age and death.

If you want to relax in peace as the dream fades or as your life ends, then learn to trust the openness that remains.

You are this openness that feels.

Rather than waiting for death, practice relaxing as this openness now.

Do this three-part exercise whenever you are ready:

1. Close your eyes, relax, and smile as you begin to fall into the blissfulness of silent, dark, deep sleep.

2. While continuing to feel this blissful nothingness, also allow thoughts and daydreams of elephants (or your workday) to move in your mind, feeling their texture, sound, and light, as if in a dream.

3. Then, open your eyes to the waking world, without losing touch with sleep's nothingness or your inner dreaminess.

By practicing this three-part exercise of falling into the bliss-place of sleep so your lips smile, while feeling your monkey-like daydreams lit up before your eye-of-mind, while also opening your physical eyes to notice the world in front of your physical body, you may suddenly open beyond all three states: waking, dreaming, and sleeping.

While practicing to feel all three states simultaneously, right now, you may suddenly realize something startling: Nothing lasts. Nothing is necessary. Nothing ever was necessary.

Your life does not need to be noticed. At death, your present life will vanish, like a dream fading away, noticed or not.

Openness is always here, holding the place where you can fall to sleep, or dream, or notice your slice of the waking world. Learn to trust this space where everything happens, regardless of what you do or don't notice.

Then, when things aren't noticed—like in sleep or as death fades your life—openness without objects will feel as home as it always is.

Every object and every thing, including your sense of self, will disappear from time to time. Whether you notice a self or not, openness remains.

Your worst nightmare—while waking or dreaming—will pass. Whether you notice a lingering dream or not, openness remains.

By the time you have finished reading this sentence, what was now has already passed.

Openness is eternal.

●

SLUT

Remember a time when you were a child and did something bad.

Maybe you were caught stealing candy or being sexual. Maybe you lied.

Feel the incident as if it were happening now. Feel naughtiness in your body. Feel your childhood guilt and excitement in your belly, heart, and head.

Now, allow this memory to dissolve or fade, right in the place it is happening.

If you turn off a slide projector, a screen remains when the image fades.

When a thought or memory fades, what remains?

Feel this openness in which your thoughts and memories show and go. When any specific thought or memory dissolves, what is left but a feeling-openness?

Instant enlightenment is to be openness, whatever shows and goes.

We close down when we resist something that doesn't seem to be love. Therefore, whenever we find ourselves resisting, we have an opportunity to open unlove into love.

Imagine someone you really don't like. Now, imagine that your purpose in life is to help that person become the most loving person possible. And now apply this to every person you know, especially those who seem so unloving.

Instead of closing to what seems unloving, we learn to open to what we would rather avoid.

Our true mission, the authentic purpose of our life, comes through us spontaneously when we open as everyone.

Love is open as everyone. You are this love, this feeling-openness, showing as everyone, including those you don't like.

Thus, if you particularly resist being a naughty person—perhaps due to a childhood memory—then you can be pretty sure that your life's purpose involves expressing love in ways more naughty than you are comfortable with.

Your fullest gift of love may be capped by your fear, frozen under a resistance to being naughty, accumulated as a child. Ask your lover this: Would he or she occasionally prefer that you were *more naughty during sex in a loving and sensitive way?* Your lover may be waiting for you to be more sexually nasty. Your lover may actually require your ravishing love, your passionate-yet-sensitive savagery, to surrender open and love more fully.

But if you are afraid to love savagely, you deny this opportunity to your lover.

The secret to gifting your life's deepest purpose is to open through what you most resist, so your love's mission can bless the world—untrapped by your accumulated history of memories.

Every past moment has evaporated. Notice what you remember, and let it go, to live free as love.

Your life's purpose is liberated by your willingness to be love, especially through the qualities you most resist in others.

Consider this: What did your parents do that made you feel, "I'll never be that way when I am grown"?

Let's imagine that your father was afraid to be vulnerable and always told everyone how to do things the correct way. He unfeelingly expounded the right way to live, whether people were open to receiving him or not.

Now, as an adult, you can remember how much you hated when he did that. You tell yourself that you'll never be as presumptuous and righteous as he was. You won't be an unfeeling know-it-all, trying to tell people how to live their lives.

You can be pretty sure, in this case, that you were born to teach people how to live their lives.

Why? Because your present birth gives you the precise obstacles you must overcome in order to give your deepest gift.

Instead of fighting with the obstacles, you learn to be love in their very form.

In this case, you might gather a few friends and tell them that you are going to do an exercise. Then, proceed to tell them how to live their lives, in exactly the same way your father did, using the same tone of voice, gestures, vocabulary, and facial expressions. Be your know-it-all father, righteously expounding the right way to live, with one exception: Stay connected to your listeners in love.

While talking, moving, and acting like your stiff and righteous know-it-all father, also feel your listeners' hearts. Feel whether your audience is opening or closing in response to your pronouncements. Notice if they are fidgeting or relaxed. Feel into their hearts and bodies with the same openness you would offer to your lover during the most vulnerable and sensitive sex—and continue expounding, on and on, the right way to live.

In other words, be love in the form you have most resisted: your righteous know-it-all father. Your deepest gift—your true life's work— is awaiting your capacity to open through the obstacles that you would rather avoid.

What seems like something negative—your naughty sex acts of your childhood, or your father's righteous know-it-all attitude—is actually the very vehicle you must lovingly inhabit for the obstruction to dissolve. Then, your spontaneous gift can be given.

"I'll never be like that" is a signpost pointing to where your most potent love—your life's mission—is buried under avoidance.

Suppose you see another woman who is dressed like a vamp, and you think to yourself, "What a slut! I wouldn't be caught dead dressed like that."

Love is openness, no resistance. If you want to liberate your deepest gifts, practice dressing like a slut while opening to offer your genuine love.

Again, you can gather with some close friends. Dress like a slut. Wear exactly what you most resist—your friends can enjoy helping you adorn yourself with the outfit, makeup, and jewelry that really evoke your nauseous resistance.

Then, acting as a slut, look into your friends' eyes, feeling into their souls. Offer love to your friends—through dance, hugs, song, or touch—your heart's most juicy expression.

Love can be wrathful, joyous, or slutty, because love is the openness that shows and goes as all possible emotions, thoughts, people, objects, and events. You are love, and thus you are all.

If you want to freely offer your heart's deepest gift—your true life's purpose—then learn to love in the styles you most resist. Previously suppressed love will be liberated.

How to start? As always, relax.

In any moment of stress, close your eyes and relax enough to feel the bliss of being deeply asleep. This is the first step out of the suppressive habit of avoiding love's expression through the styles, people, and emotions that you resist.

Continue with the exercise. Fall into deep, blissful nothingness, and also allow thoughts and daydreams to hover in your mind, feeling their motion, texture, and luminosity. Then, open your eyes to the waking world, without losing touch with sleep's nothingness or your mind's dreamy meanderings.

When you are successful at this— feeling right now where you are sleeping, dreaming, and awake, all at the same time—then feel your physical body as it is.

Perhaps you are sitting or standing. If sitting, your legs may be crossed; your feet may be propped on a stool or flat on the floor. Your jaw and belly may be soft or tense. Your throat may be swallowing.

Your breathing may be deep or shallow. Your hair may be cut short or sweeping across your face and shoulders.

In any case, feel yourself as you are, right now, as you read these words.

Whatever you feel of yourself "right now" is a memory—modern science could describe the required time for your nervous system to ooze and spark as electrochemical impulses traveled from your sense organs to your brain.

Your so-called present experience of yourself right now is but a memory trace of the "you" that has already happened, similar to your memory of being bad as a child.

What you perceive "right now" is
alive and alight like a dreamworld.

What is your *direct* experience of the
whole picture right now?

Close your eyes and slowly open
them, repeatedly, until you can
effortlessly feel the imagery of
the "outside world" as a vision,
an electronic show, like a movie
projected in midair.

Where, exactly, is this midair?

Is it the same openness that remains
where your memories and dreamy
images dissolve away?

Whether you are issuing edicts like your know-it-all father, frowning at a sluttishly dressed woman, or hugging and dancing with your friends while you are dressed as a vamp, this openness is still here, full of feeling whatever you are feeling.

This openness has always been you. Try remembering before you were born. Take a moment right now and relax, feeling into the past as far as you can. Feel before your earliest memories as a toddler or an infant. Do you hit a hard wall, or do you feel an ineffable, formless openness before your earliest memories?

Is this the same blissful nothingness into which you fall during deep sleep?

Find out.

Thinking about these things won't help. Really feel into the openness before you were born. Feel into the place where you can fall deeply asleep, right now.

If you fall open and completely let go, a sudden sigh occurs: You are this openness. You can *be* blissful openness, but you can't *get* there.

So, instead of trying to *view* it, relax open *as* this ever-present background of feeling-openness. Take care not to *seek* blissfulness as an aspect of your true self. Who you truly are is an openness of love in which bliss may or may not be noticed.

In this openness, all qualities may or may not be noticed—the naughty child, the pompous father, the slutty vamp—dancing as love's shapes before being forgotten. Openness remains.

Who you truly are is this feeling-openness. So let go of each experience as instantly as it occurs.

Again and again, allow your actual sensations—itches, aches, warmth—to dissolve where they are noticed.

Allow your body image—the outline formed by your skin, whether you feel fat or thin—to dissolve open.

Feeling lonely, victorious, or worshipped? Let go so that each noticing—every thought—dissolves on its own, vanishing in the openness where it is first felt.

If you repeat this exercise continuously, your behaviors will emerge as love's unfettered action. You won't feel trapped by a past or a future—even the present is happening-to-gone in the middle of nowhere, wide open and free.

This freedom from time is love.

You were born to offer this love in the style you would most avoid. Every moment that you face, every person that you meet, provides you with an opportunity to live as love.

Is this true? Do this experiment and find out.

Remember seeing a person and saying to yourself, "I'll never be like that." The experiment is to practice *being love* exactly like that—in the style you swore you would never be like—over and over, until the past no longer scrimps the depth of love's spontaneous offering.

You are part of the natural evolution of love's offering, including your community of loved ones. Tell them how to live their lives just like your father expounded—but while truly feeling their hearts. Offer them the delight of your show-off slutty style—but while breathing their sorrow as yours. Be naughty—but always as love extending tenderly, without separating into a private world of guilt.

Love wants to come through you most in the styles you want to express the least. Otherwise, you would already be living utterly spontaneously, gifting the world through your true purpose, without inhibition or doubt, while always letting go as unfettered openness.

Let go so each noticing dissolves on its own, vanishing in the openness where it first appears.

Where has every thought gone that has ever been noticed?

Relax as this place of openness.

As openness, offer love into the picture where you find your body and mind moving with others, especially in the styles that you resist.

Holding back hurts.

You suffer because you have so far refused to open as every style of love. You are love, and love is all.

Notice who you would never want to be like, offer love in their style you so resist, and then let your memory of the moment dissolve open to where all noticing goes.

Including this one.

PARENTS

Imagine your parents having sex.
They did, you know.

You were born because your parents
had sex. This is obvious.

But consider this possibility: you were
born specifically to learn to offer love
as the very form you inherited from
your parents.

Imagine yourself, or your soul if you like, hovering wherever souls abide before they are born in human form. Imagine choosing to become embodied because you need to feel loved, sexually pleasured, successful, or secure, just like the forces that moved your parents to come together, perform intercourse, create your bodily form, and earn enough money to feed you.

If you need to experience or know anything—if you require time to gain any sense of fulfillment—then you require a birth that unfolds the lessons that will allot you the opportunity to live free as love's openness. You are the continuation of your parents' unlearned lessons, unless you are totally and absolutely free right now.

What were the worst qualities of your mother and father?

Imagine your parents' worst qualities having sex together, trying to merge with each other to be relieved of themselves.

Perhaps your father wanted to feel respected, and he needed to be relieved of tension, so he lusted to ejaculate in your mother: of this you were born.

Perhaps your mother's heart so yearned to be seen and appreciated by your father, she opened her body to him, full of need, frustration, and hope: of this you were born.

Regardless of your inheritance, your mission by birth is to love. That's why your life will present you with the opportunity to open and love while you repeatedly face your parents' worst qualities, until your heart can stay relaxed, open as the sky is wide.

Your life will offer you many opportunities to love while facing your parents' negative qualities.

You may find yourself struggling with your emotionally distant father in the face of your lover's emotional pull-back.

The under-appreciation you felt as a child may continually show up in adulthood as your colleagues belittling your work, or the world failing to recognize your art.

You may face your parents' qualities in your own character, as they have been passed to you through your ancestral lineage of sexual couplings.

Whatever your inheritance of personal need, you can commit to doing your best to open, permitting love's force to freely move your life.

Spontaneously gift the world and your beloveds from your deepest heart, right now, even as you continue to face your parents' unfulfilled desires in yourself and others.

Assume that your born life was designed as an opportunity to love freely in spite of your parents' worst qualities.

How do you grow free in your offering of love?

Start by loving your parents—and their worst qualities—with gratitude for creating your body.

Offer the most love to whatever most disturbs you—in your parents, yourself, or others.

Practice to offer love, just as you are. You may be angry, but you can still offer love in angry form to a lover who is playing out his or her inherited traits of deceitfulness or self-centered pleasurizing.

Love can be textured through anger—or any emotion—as long as your heart remains connected to and open with your lover's.

Now is your chance to use your specific birth as an opportunity to offer love regardless of your inheritance of wounds. Assume that learning to love—even when you also feel rage, jealousy, or fear—is one of the main reasons you are here, born as you are, appearing in your specific world of relationships.

You can be a free offering of love, in spite of your genealogical shortcomings, your habits of emotion, and everyone else's.

You don't have to close when you hurt. You can be hurt and remain open, allowing your pain to be felt by others along with your love, offered through your unguarded, torn heart. This is your gift of love, in the midst of your inherited emotional damage and endowments.

Your parents gave you a precise form and momentum; your task is to discover that what they gave you is precisely sufficient to open as love, without waiting for anything else at all. You can offer love now. No excuses.

Most people wait to give their love. They feel that something has been missing in their lives, ever since their childhood. They are hoping to get, not to give.

Everybody feels this same sense of lack. It's not personal. It's what everyone is born to love through.

This feeling of "love's lack" is only a test: Will you close and wait, or can you offer your open heart even while sensing that something is missing?

Your parents have given you the opportunity of a lifetime.

Bless your parents for giving you an inherited drama that perpetuates itself, giving you time and frustration so you can learn to offer love now, without waiting.

Your parents' worst qualities, which probably played a large part in sexually uniting them for the sake of your birth, are your special springboard from which to offer love.

Alcohol may have stripped your parents of inhibition and clothing. Bless the alcohol that originated you, so that you may love others in the midst of their pain.

Spite may have spurred your mother to cheat on her boyfriend, resulting in your birth. Bless spite, for it has created you as a means by which love can infuse the world.

Pornography may have excited biological passion, and nine months later your body emerged from your mother's. Bless pornography for the inspiration that mingled the procreative fluids resulting in your body reading these words, so that you may serve others.

You can now choose to be moved by an inherited sense of lack, or you can bless all and everyone, and move on.

Let go of the old story of your life.

Whatever has pained you the most, bless it for spurring you on to learn the way of offering love amidst hurt.

Live and die free of past cause,
loving open, future unknown, forever.

This is instant enlightenment.

ASS

Scratch your ass. Go ahead, if you are alone, scratch your buttocks, near the crack. You've done it before, probably many times. Just do it now so you can remember the feeling well.

Now, imagine you are a butterfly. A butterfly can see and fly, but it can't scratch its ass. A butterfly will never know how it feels to scratch its ass.

Say the word "cow."

A worm will never experience
speaking this word as you just have.

The fact that you are currently human
means that your set of experiences
is severely circumscribed, just as is a
worm's or a butterfly's.

Liberating yourself from this human-
only view allows the scope of your
love to include all beings. Instant
enlightenment means to love and be
open to feel *all*, now.

Try an experiment. Pretend you are
another creature, so you are familiar
with another, non-human world.

Imagine that you are a bacterium
living in your neighbor's intestines.
Let's call your neighbor "Joe."

Joe experiences his lounge chair like you would the lining of Joe's gut. Imagine feeding in Joe's mucosal membranes just as Joe might be hunkering down into a chair to have a drink.

If Joe drinks a few shots of tequila, he drenches thousands of your offspring and other innocent members of your community in noxious alcohol. Really feel this happening, as you and your relatives are soaked in toxic liquid.

You may be human, but there are plenty of non-humans who suffer pain and death that you don't even notice.

Humans are neither at the top nor at the bottom of the heap. Fashion trends are larger than an individual human life. Imagine you are a fashion trend spreading through human culture, showing up in restaurants, magazines, movies, and TV shows.

Imagine you are a great idea—like the notion of Christianity or the belief that antibiotics can be created to eradicate some diseases.

You would gestate for a while before taking birth as a clear idea spelled out fully at a specific time in history, morphing through a life lasting centuries. Eventually, your power would wear thin, with every new idea, discovery, or innovation rendering you more impotent and less fertile, no longer as useful.

Having traveled through many countries and crossed many hundreds of years, you would disappear, your obituary perhaps a paragraph in a history book, as the next generation of great ideas are born and traverse the globe, replacing your reign.

While still a viable idea, humans sustain your life in vibrating rhythms of writing and speech, patterning and evolving as myths or scientific theories that hold together for a while, much like the hum of crickets rising and falling in dramatic crescendos. Finally, you are outmoded and replaced, whether you are the notion of a flat earth or a fire god.

And the newest ideas always think they are most true.

Your actual human life is larger than a bacterium's, smaller than that of the idea of Christianity, and pretty much the same as other humans'.

Therefore, your love is often limited to feeling the human sphere of values. You naturally spend most of your time in the drama of you-and-other-humans, synchronized by lifespan.

Your love is less tuned into the community needs of bacteria, or the dreadful time that Christianity must be experiencing right now as it faces commercial televangelism and wanton scandals.

We share love with those who seem like us. We feel their pain. We try to make peace with our "own" kind, one of our defining features being that we all scratch our asses, unlike butterflies and religious ideas.

Instant enlightenment is to love and feel all, every animal, plant, rainstorm, and idea. Even space itself. Love the *entire* display as a spontaneous emanation of openness and light.

Act as a human, but love and feel all.

We have no problem destroying the AIDS virus, just as the virus has no problem destroying us; our life-dramas are intertwined, though the virus doesn't know your dying father's kindness and you don't know the virus's sense of frantic replication.

Love is the willingness to feel what it would be to exist as a virus, harvesting human cells so you can replicate, so your offspring can continue as the next generation.

Kill if you must, but do so while loving, not fearing. Allow love to guide your actions in relation to all beings, some of which we harvest to eat or to make our shoes, just as we are harvested by others for their use.

What happens if you relax all stressful concern for reproduction and self-preservation for just a few seconds, and directly discover what happens when *only* love for all is allowed to move you?

How do humans treat the earth and all its inhabitants if we help each other to always feel the entirety of love's luminous display, large and small?

If just two people live together this way, what kind of communication ensues?

If a community relaxes as this trust of love, open without knowing what is to appear, how will love show in our interwoven lives?

As a human, you might still scratch your ass.

You know that one day you will suffer and die.

So what does love do as you feel the harvest and know you are helpless to the sacrifice?

Answer with your life.

Die fully given.

LAZY

Be as lazy as possible. Commit to absolute laziness. Don't do anything that you don't have to do. Just lie on the floor.

Don't breathe, unless you can't help it. Don't blink, unless it happens by itself. Don't think, unless thoughts occur despite your best efforts not to do anything.

Be utterly lazy, and then do whatever you find yourself doing, as an offering for others. For instance, if a blink happens, feel the blink as a work of art, offered outwardly for love's sake. If others were to see you blink, they would feel, "Now, *that* is a beautiful blink."

Eventually, you will need to get up off the floor to pee. Or, maybe you will be so lazy that you'll just pee where you are, in a growing pond of your own urine. In any case, pee as art, as an offering, as love's gift. This example probably seems exaggerated, but everything you do *is* love's gift, unless you are unwilling to be lived by love's force.

Do nothing, but if doing happens, do it as love's most fully offered art. This disposition is instant enlightenment: nothing happening but love.

Living any other way is suffering. Have you noticed?

You are actively participating in an interconnected chain of opposition, struggle, and destruction. For you to read these words, computer chips and plastics were probably produced in less-developed countries by men and women paid barely-living wages in factories dumping toxic byproducts into our shared atmosphere and water.

You are a link in a chain of suffering that affords you the luxury of reading these words. It's not your fault, but it is your responsibility.

Perfect freedom—unadulterated laziness—is perfect responsibility. Rather than self-interest or personal desire, love moves you when you are too lazy to move yourself. Love *is* responsibility.

You owe it to all beings to commit to laziness, absolutely. Be so lazy that choice disappears. Only a singularity remains that moves you. Love.

The only way to break the chain of suffering built of self-interest is to allow the singularity of love to do your actions, words, and thoughts.

Do nothing, except what you *must* do because love has its way through your body and mind.

This may necessitate raising a family and achieving a high-paying career, or it may require becoming a monk in India or a tree-cutter in the Amazonian jungles.

Discover love's means. Add nothing personal. Too lazy to act on self-interest, how does love move you? This is instant enlightenment, although you probably don't believe it.

Keep trying, until you're tired of trying, and then trust love's bursting through your body and mind. Commit to perfect laziness, giving up choice, adding nothing to what love *makes* you do, spontaneously.

●

OUTWARD

The typical human experience is that awareness is *in here* and space is *out there*.

But this isn't your actual experience right now. Feel: Where is awareness located?

You may have a certain sensation in your head or heart, but where is the awareness that is aware of that sensation?

Feeling right now, awareness is spread evenly throughout the open sphere of experience. Space is awareness.

What happens when you relax awareness, so it isn't fixated upon any particular thought or thing? What happens when you feel space without grasping it in any way?

What happens when you place unfixated awareness in supportless space?

Actually do this for as long as it lasts, like striking a bell once, so it rings, sustaining a sound in space for a while.

Eventually, awareness retracts or fixates on something. Then, strike the bell again, gently placing unfixated awareness in supportless space, and let it sustain wide open effortlessly, until awareness fixates on something: a thought, an emotion, a memory. Again, allow relaxed awareness to be placed in supportless space, like a bell's ring openly pervading the air.

Awareness isn't felt to be inside, while space is assumed to be out there. Rather, awareness permeates space— space is alive and full as awareness.

Instant enlightenment is like this: awareness ringing open as space.

●

SPEECH

"Hello, good to see you."

This sentence can be said with the energy of anger, sweetness, sexiness, hatefulness, or coyness.

You can speak with any energetic quality, pervading the concert hall of your experience. The bodies in this hall—yours and others'—are resonated by the energy you offer.

Choose the energy of your speech like a musician selecting a song from his or her repertoire, for the sake of opening the audience.

Enlightenment is responsibility.

Be responsible for your breathing, your posture, your thoughts, and your speech, artfully opening those who float in this moment of appearance with you.

Allow your awareness to pervade the colors and shapes of your experience. Spreading awareness in space, include the bodies of others. Your speech-energy instantly pervades these bodies, and everyone feels it.

How responsible are you willing to be? The world awaits your answer, like an audience at your concert.

ROMANCE

The next time you feel attracted to someone, imagine having fantastic sex with him or her (or exchanging suggestive glances during a candlelight dinner, or sliding against one another in a warm bath, or cavorting together under a waterfall—whatever your fantasy might be).

Try doing this all day. If you are attracted to your boss or colleague, fantasize about him or her. Fantasize about sexy strangers on the street or at the grocery store, or even about actors and actresses on TV or the movie screen.

Once you can actively and freely fantasize in this way, do the following series of exercises. You can perform one or two that work best for you, or rotate them, one after another, with every person you find attractive:

1. Whatever your fantasy is (savage sex in a steamy jungle, gentle massage in the lapping waters of a warm beach), see and feel your fantasy like a movie. Speed up the movie, faster and faster. Speed it up until it is a blur of white light.

2. Start the fantasy wherever you naturally do (imagining you are in a canopied bed surrounded by candles, or behind a bush in a public park), and continue the fantasy, at fast speed, imagining the rest of your lives together.

   Fantasize growing old together, your attractive partner rotting with age: teeth falling out, breasts sagging like pancakes, penis shriveling like a worm, breath stinking like mold.

Repeat this over and over for a few minutes, starting with the sexy fantasy and proceeding through inevitable old age, disease, and decrepitude.

End each fantasy with you or your imagined partner dying, putrid excretions dribbling from every hole.

3. Engage your favorite fantasy, but with a kind of X-ray vision, so your partner's skin becomes transparent.

You might still be together,
dancing beneath the moonlight
or making love in the woods, but
now see your lover's intestines,
bile, lymph, skeleton, and liver.
Your lover's bladder fills with urine
while your lover's colon lurches
with excrement.

Continue the fantasy for a few
minutes as if you had this kind of
X-ray vision, seeing right through
the skin to what your attractive
lover really looks like on the
inside.

4. Modern physics explains that
matter is energy. Even flesh
and bones are mostly space,
with widely separated particles
vibrating as probabilities. So,
imagine your favorite fantasy,

feeling your body and your lover's as mostly space vibrating: space making love with space, energy dancing with energy, in a meadow of flowers or on a fluffy blanket that is also space vibrating as energy.

5. Remember all the times you have experienced a "great moment" in the past, romantically or sexually. What has it come to, now?

   Although the memory may be wonderful to hold in your mind as you reminisce, has your mostly constant sense of loneliness, despair, or sorrow fundamentally changed because of it?

Fantasize fully—with musky smells, sinful pleasures, sensual ravishing, and luscious tastes— feeling the fantasy dissolve to nothing on the spot. Instantly.

Repeat: Feel the full, fleshed-out fantasy immediately dissolving to insignificance, as all your great moments have in the past. Go back and forth between vivid fantasy and vanishment-into-openness until you are uninterested in continuing.

These five exercises can be done with any actual moment of experience, not only your fantasies.

Suddenly, it is obvious: every great moment—remembered or hoped for—is lavishly alive and full of life's richness, and also empty, vanished, and forgotten without a trace.

When these two feelings—fullness and emptiness—are simultaneous and instant, your life is free and an expression of love. No hope, memory, or fantasy is needed or indulged. And if a thought or fantasy *is* indulged, simply repeat these exercises.

Of course, as long as you choose momentary great experiences over the ever-present surrender as love's spontaneous expression, you'll refuse these exercises.

A dreadfully routine life peppered with a few great moments. Or, the ever-explosive and singular offering of your heart's deepest love. It's your choice.

●

RADIO

While listening to the radio, try to locate where you hear the sound of music.

You might think the sound is "inside my head." But you can't really feel a border bounded by your skull, can you?

When hearing happens, sound occurs in a space with no specific borders. Where is this space in which sound occurs? Where does it feel to be?

Hearing is to be aware of sound. The space of sound is the same space as the awareness of sound. Awareness and space are one openness.

All sensations—smell, touch, sight, taste, and sound—come and go, but the potential space where they happen is an ever-present openness. Dreams come and go in this place at night, and so does music from the radio, and everything you are experiencing right now.

Notice while listening to the radio that you have no sense of your head's borders. What is your direct experience?

Above your shoulders, you are wide open!

Openness is where your head should be, above your shoulders. If you look down, your whole body appears in this awareness-space of openness. So, actually, your shoulders are within, not below, this openness.

But don't think about it. Directly feel what is above your shoulders. What do you feel? A bony case with peepholes through which you peer? Or, a boundless openness in which everything appears?

This may be the first time in your life that you directly feel what is above your shoulders, so please do give it a try.

This openness, this happening-place that seems above your shoulders, is actually rooted in your heart's feeling. It is like the so-called "balloon" drawn in a cartoon that holds a character's words, coming not from your lips as in most cartoons, but coming from your heart.

In your case, this openness-balloon has no borders. Everything you experience occurs within it. And, although the openness seems to be a space above your shoulders, its source is in your heart.

Therefore, what you hear on the radio—all your experience—touches your heart. Be the openness you are; everything and everyone touches your heart. The happening-place of every possible experience is your heart's feeling-openness, filled with perceptions, that seems to float as open space above your shoulders.

Nothing and nobody is separate from your heart's feeling capacity. This openness of feeling is the space where you hear the radio, where you think and dream, and where these words appear right now. Feel this openness where your head should be, these words now appearing and instantly touching your heart: I love you.

●

CHANT

Chanting is halfway between speaking and singing. *Speak* a single tone—"Ah"—in your normal speaking voice. Now, *sing* the same tone. You will feel a difference. Chanting is to sing in your speaking voice.

Chant "Ah" with every exhalation for about five minutes. Feel "Ah" spreading outward, pervading space, and dissolving in openness. Eventually, add variations in pitch. Use various shapings of your lips, tongue, and jaw to produce different sounds. And finally, allow *words* to be shaped from the "Ah."

All words are modifications of a universal tone, modulations of the space-pervading "Ah."

Chanting allows you to open love's space in your heart.

Chant "Ah" until you feel your heart open, love's sound offering outward to all, and beyond.

Feel how word-forms take shape,
like waves in love's openness.

"Ah" is the openness of love. Words
are its textures.

While speaking, feel each word *and*
the universal "Ah" love-tone of which
it is a modulation.

Feel "Ah" as open love. Speak all
words as shapes tongued from the
openness of your heart's devotion.

Devotional speech is modulating
"Ah" so that every word released
from your lips carries love, opening
as space without end.

●

HERO

You consider certain people to be
your heroes. Perhaps your hero
is a movie star or sports player.
Or maybe your hero is a scientist
or politician. You may have lesser
heroes like your grandmother and
greater heroes like Jesus, Mother
Mary, Martin Luther King, Jr., or the
Dalai Lama.

The reason someone is your hero is
because he or she embodies qualities
of divinity. Your hero is a vehicle
through which goodness, truth, or
beauty shines.

But if these qualities weren't already alive in you, then you wouldn't resonate with them in your heroes. It takes one to know one.

Instant enlightenment is to relax as the openness displaying all the heroic qualities that are your very nature—your actual possible expressions in any moment.

You can probably feel a call to evolve whispering—or shouting—in your heart. You yearn to grow, to cultivate deeper love, to develop your heart's gifts.

You feel a natural urgency toward making your life a sacred offering by becoming transparent to the divine qualities that want to shine through your life.

One way to cooperate with your heartfelt call to evolve is to relax as openness, and imagine yourself to be your hero or heroine.

Suppose that Jesus is a hero for you. First, relax your heart from the things that seem to be happening in the picture of the current moment.

As if reaching your hand into dense fog but finding nothing there, feel from your heart into awareness-space itself.

Relax the tension around your heart and ease open *as* this awareness-space, an endless sphere of feeling, where all the world and you are happening now.

Actually feel—and allow yourself to be—the openness that is awareness, shining as all the light you see, vibrating as the sound you hear, taking shape as every taste, smell, and tingle.

Relax as heart-open awareness, visualizing Jesus (or any of your heroes) vividly in front of you. Slowly, allow the image of your hero to come closer and closer, until your body and your hero's body are mingled as one.

Wear the body of Jesus, as if it were your own. Feel what it would be to breathe, sit, walk, or speak as your hero. Be heart-open awareness, shining as the light, vibrating as the words, and taking the shape of Jesus, your hero.

When you can feel that you are embodying all the qualities of your hero, allow the visualization to dissolve, while retaining the sense of the qualities you so admire. Relax your intentional inhabitance of Jesus' form, continuing to feel the truth, beauty, or goodness of your hero shining forth.

You can practice this same exercise with movie stars, athletes, or world leaders. Wear, feel, and express the very qualities of all your heroes.

As you develop more skill, the entire process occurs instantaneously. You visualize your hero, feel and merge with the form of your hero, and then dissolve as that form, remaining openly alive, spaciously shining as the qualities you admire.

Whenever you feel an enlightened or divine quality in a person, you can relax open as that quality, instantly, through this exercise.

Then, in the display of your life, you can offer this quality as a gift to others, as you embody it more deeply. Eventually, the visualization becomes unnecessary. Without effort, you are an open force of blessing.

Relaxed as openness itself, you spontaneously offer the gifts of all your heroes and heroines.

●

BETTER

Wanting to become better is quite natural. Seeking perfection—in love or art—is an aspect of the evolutionary force that lives through everyone.

This desire to be outstanding, and to give whatever gifts you can to others, is the birthright of every human being. Yet, most people are too afraid or lazy to achieve their goals and serve others fully.

Nevertheless, to do so—to live an outstanding life—is nothing great.

Imagine a world of super achievers and gifters.

Suppose everyone on earth is like Bill Gates, a multi-billionaire supporting numerous charities. Or perhaps the population is like Nelson Mandela or Oprah Winfrey, overcoming imprisonment or abuse to achieve freedom and success, offering the same opportunity to many others.

In this imaginary world, everyone is getting what they want and giving all they can for the benefit of others.

As all things do, this imaginary world would pass, as beautiful as it may be. Everyone in this world would die, sooner or later, possibly in peace during sleep, or possibly in great suffering due to an excruciating disease or unexpected accident. The earth itself isn't going to last all that long, in the cosmic scheme of things.

Even while alive, what would these super achievers and gifters find if they inspected the all-ness of any moment closely?

Using every instrument in the arsenal of modern science, most of everything remains unknown—there are more massive galaxies and subatomic realms that we can't see than we can.

So, in this imaginary, perfect world of outstanding beings in the midst of a mysterious universe, what is the best that we can hope for before the sun dies out?

Perhaps global peace. The end of starvation and untreated diseases for all humans. Magnificent art.

Imagine that you inhabit this as-perfect-as-possible world. Your friends and family share unobstructed love with you until they die. Money, food, and energy are plentiful—let's assume we've learned to create pollution-free, renewable energy sources.

We share our abundance with all humans and as many non-humans as possible, too, protecting and enriching our earthly environment.

You live in beauty, goodness, and truth, and you are in awe at all that lies beyond your capacity to know, too.

So, what exactly do you do with your life?

Perhaps you spend your lifetime producing wonderful paintings, symphonies, philosophical tracts, homes, parks, space vehicles, sexual relationships, or a family—anything and everything you want.

The comfort of this kind of world would be tremendously seductive. That is, you would pay attention to what appears as "you and the world" because it would be so immensely pleasurable to do so.

But how long would you remain satisfied?

An evolutionary impulse is at work in our appearing world. You can see it in the fossil records and throughout recorded human history. You can see it reflected in the lives of individuals, growing from infancy to adulthood.

And you can feel it very immediately in your sense of dissatisfaction— even if you lived an outstanding life in a perfect world.

We are aspects of a whole that seems to want to become *more* whole. The perfect world we have been describing is at best a phase in the growth of such an evolutionary impulse.

Your life now may be more comfortable and beautiful than that of most people still struggling on Earth. Yet, if the evolutionary impulse is alive in you, so is dissatisfaction.

An outstanding life is not always the same as an authentically deep one. In fact, if you ask some people, you will discover that many of their deepest learnings came in times of great suffering, despair, loss, scarcity, and frustrated desire.

When you outgrow something, you know it. Whatever you outgrow becomes less interesting to you.

Our comfortable world of abundance, of shared success and generous giving, would eventually become uninteresting, in the way that brushing your teeth is. You continue doing it because it feels good and you know it is good for you; you teach your children to brush their teeth because you care for their well-being. But you don't live for the sake of brushing your teeth. You have evolved beyond that.

In the same way, there will come a time when you no longer live for the sake of improving your own life, sharing harmony while relieving suffering in the world and serving others. You may continue performing these actions, but more as a good habit—like brushing your teeth—and less as a reason to live.

Released of the motivating force of living an outstanding life and helping others to do so, too, your attention literally relaxes from things—all things, including yourself and others.

Your attention naturally ceases to be highly motivated toward or away from anything or anyone.

You neither seek nor try not to seek, even as the evolutionary impulse lives through you.

Every moment spontaneously appears and disappears— instantaneously, forever.

Suddenly, an inversion occurs. Since it happens in a way to which words can only point, any explanation of this instant enlightenment falls short.

It is as if nothing has ever happened.

Yet, everything continues to happen, moved by the evolutionary impulse.

This is the beginning of a different kind of life altogether. As this vista deepens, birth and death may no longer even be noticed or remembered.

So few people seem to have exhausted their desire for "better" that very few models exist for a life lived from the perspective-free openness of being. Many people have come to a point of despair, even those who have lived outstanding lives. But few have allowed their despair to infiltrate so deeply that hope and fear fade in always-sudden openness.

Even fewer people have demonstrated what it is to live a human life in time *as* this openness, through which the evolutionary impulse displays.

Would you just sit and die? Would you create song and dance? Would you live sexually or celibately?

Why don't you find out, starting now?

Or, continue to seek ways of improving yourself and serving the world as a reason for living, until, like brushing your teeth, the evolutionary impulse is lived, but hardly as a reason to go on living it.

This is the course of enlightenment
for those who are moved to improve
self and world:

Live an outstanding life and give
what you can for the sake of others,
as your personal motivation naturally
diminishes toward zero.

Then, relax through the inevitable
phase of despair until you fabricate
no value for being alive.

With nothing left to gain or lose,
offer yourself to be lived as the
singular expression of love's
evolutionary force.

Act and offer spontaneously,
instantly open, gone as a bright
dream forgotten, appearing and
never happening, just as it is.

Deep in your heart is humor, giving space for this divine paradox of unity: love's bright and unstoppable offering at one with time's yearning to vanish as sudden openness.

Live free as love.

●

BULGE

Slowly, open and close your eyelids. Notice that even though the colors come and go, the capacity for light remains. As you open and close your eyes, pay attention to what *doesn't* change.

Put your hands over your ears, covering them to block out most sound, then remove your hands so you can hear again. Repeat this, and notice what stays while sound comes and goes.

Hold your breath until you feel that you can't anymore, and then breathe. A feeling of anxiety—the need to breathe—builds up as you hold your breath, and then it disappears when you breathe again. Notice the ever-present openness of awareness that is able to feel, even as anxiety comes and goes.

When you have practiced these exercises with your eyes, ears, and breath long enough, you will know ever-present openness easily. This openness is alive and familiar. You *are* this openness—seeing, hearing, and feeling.

Learn to trust this ever-present openness until you can let go wide open, throwing out the contents of every moment just as the sun throws out light.

Holding to nothing, fall open as the unsupported space of boundless feeling, radiating outward.

Almost instantly, a collapse occurs: "I'm hungry." "My rent is due." "Am I truly loved for who I am?"

Again, relax open and feel without end.

Whatever you think or perceive, radiate your experience as a luminous display projecting in the openness of space.

When you do this, the presence of openness spontaneously begins to bulge forth.

You act not as a solid, separate person, but as love's open offering.

Offer this bulging openness to others. Feel openness intensifying, moving toward and entering other people.

If you were bulging openness toward and into characters of a dream, their luminosity would brighten as if you were turning up the shine of their presence.

Eventually, the intensity of the dream-light itself would become more obvious than any particular image in the dream, including all the dreamt people and your own dreamt self.

The same is true now. This place that you call "now" is lit up and present, just like a dream world. You can allow the luminosity and presence of you and everyone to bulge forth, opening as everything.

The universe is naturally expanding open, just as you are. This intensity of openness saturates and pervades all that is happening.

At first, effort is required to feel this openness, because you are used to constricting attention to what's happening: your incessant thoughts, your boyfriend's wandering eye, your girlfriend's ass. But these things *are* the bulging feeling of being, rippling as shapes, like a movie projected in space, the action occurring in midair.

Difficult to describe in words, but unmistakable in direct experience. Simply close and open your eyes, cover and uncover your ears, hold your breath until anxious, then breathe again. Whatever has remained constant through all of this is the openness that feels.

Bulge it.

Radiate without limit, intensifying your offering, the openness that feels.

What scientists call the "big bang" is an offering; the expanding universe is love's impulse to saturate all space with feeling.

Be a big bang of love, offering unending openness like an ever-expanding ocean without shores. Saturate and pervade all others as if they were dry sponges, and soak them open in the liquid light of love, until they bulge, full of feeling, too.

The more you offer this bulge of ever-present openness to others, the more the display that includes you soaks full as a love-swelled offering.

Your loving is a gift to others. Your light ignites theirs. Your bulging presence intensifies their heart's fullness, which is an openness of *feeling*, filled with light, sound, and pulsing emotion.

Throw out feeling-openness like the sun's rays filling space.

Offer your feeling-presence, bulging open without effort.

Relax as you bulge, as if melting into your lover and bursting open.

The rest will happen by itself.

Being is bulging.

Feeling is bulging.

All unnecessary suffering is the
refusal to bulge as love's offering.

AGE

Infants don't dream of having sex with the waitress. Most eighty-year-olds don't obsess about being tied down and tongue-tortured above the knees.

Although there are exceptions, sexual desire, as a bodily experience, belongs mostly to the middle years of life.

They make a big deal about it, those mid-year bipeds, jazzed to seduce and impress. They sometimes play up the sex, and other times play it down. They use the mirror in their bathroom as a sexual reflection. Their shopping for clothes is riddled with sexual motivation. They walk and stand and glance for the purpose. They dab themselves with scents of arousal.

For your middle years, sex is a powerful bodily force; so influential, even your present hairstyle was probably chosen, in part, for sexual reasons. Yet, how good has sex really been for you?

Considering its almost-constant determining influence in your mid-years, how many total hours—or minutes—have truly been worth the time, money, pain, and effort you have put into sexing it up?

The play is pleasurable, of course, whether you get laid or not. But obviously the payoff isn't in the sex itself, which for most people is too quick, shallow, and eventually humdrum, if you stay with the same partner long enough.

The true payoff, if you play for real, is this: bodily sex prepares you to make love as each moment's passion—open, want-free oneness playing as desire-driven multiplicity.

Just as the sky can't be separated from its blue appearance, yet is not itself blue, openness can't be other than passionate happening, yet is not itself happening.

This is sex: you want something other than now, and yet only the surrender of that desire allows its fulfillment.

And so through the mid-years, the game plays for its own sake. Yes, give it to me. No, I don't want it. Sex.

With advancing years, the games of sex seem silly. You know of youth spent in pursuit's folly.

And so it is with every moment. Now goes nowhere but now, and yet it goes and goes and goes.

Like an old dog at rest, eventually you have seen and done it all. And if you haven't, you've wasted your mid-years.

If now isn't as open as the best moments of sex in your life, then continue repeating the exercises in this book, or do whatever equalizes inside and outside so openness is alive as sex-blue space.

Is there anything preventing you from surrendering your body open, leaving nothing but the living colors of love, even as aging grants you the clear light of death?

●

LOVE

For instant enlightenment, this is the test: Can you love during ever-increasing heaven and hell?

Can you love in all directions, inwardly and outwardly?

Even during moods of disgust and pain and shame and death wishes doubling unto themselves in a tight knot of loneliness and searing torment, can you love?

If you cannot love, nothing changes.

If you can love, nothing changes.

Except that you can love.

Nothing and nobody will ever give you anything except an opportunity to love.

Now.

●

TITLES BY DAVID DEIDA

BOOKS

The Way of the Superior Man

A Spiritual Guide to Mastering the Challenges of Women, Work, and Sexual Desire

David Deida explores the most important issues in men's lives—from career and family to women and intimacy to love and sex—to offer the ultimate spiritual guide for men living a life of integrity, authenticity, and freedom.

ISBN: 978-1-59179-257-4 / US $17.95

Dear Lover

A Woman's Guide to Men, Sex, and Love's Deepest Bliss

How do you attract and keep a man capable of meeting what you most passionately yearn for? To answer this question, David Deida explores every aspect of the feminine practice of spiritual intimacy, from sexuality and lovemaking to family and career to emotions, trust, and commitment.

ISBN: 978-1-59179-260-4 / US $16.95

Blue Truth
A Spiritual Guide to Life & Death and Love & Sex

David Deida presents a treasury of skills and insights for uncovering and offering your true heart of purpose, passion, and unquenchable love.

ISBN: 978-1-59179-259-8 / US $16.95

Intimate Communion
Awakening Your Sexual Essence

David Deida's first book lays the foundation for his teaching on the integration of intimacy and authentic spiritual practice.

ISBN: 978-1-55874-374-8

Finding God Through Sex
Awakening the One of Spirit Through the Two of Flesh

No matter how much we pray or meditate, it's not always easy to integrate sexual pleasure and spiritual depth. David Deida helps single men and women and couples of every orientation turn sex into an erotic act of deep devotional surrender.

ISBN: 978-1-59179-273-4 / US $16.95

Wild Nights
Conversations with Mykonos about Passionate Love, Extraordinary Sex, and How to Open to God

Meet Mykonos—scurrilous madman, and speaker of truth. A recollection of a unique relationship between a student and an extraordinary spiritual teacher.

ISBN: 978-1-59179-233-8 / US $15.95

The Enlightened Sex Manual

Sexual Skills for the Superior Lover

The secret to enlightenment and great sex is revealed to be one and the same in this groundbreaking manual for adventurous lovers. The ultimate collection of skills for opening to the physical, emotional, and spiritual rewards of intimate embrace. Includes CD with guided practices.

ISBN: 978-1-59179-585-8 / US $15.95

It's a Guy Thing

An Owner's Manual for Women

David Deida answers over 150 of women's most asked questions about men and intimacy.

ISBN: 978-155874-464-6

AUDIO

Enlightened Sex
Finding Freedom & Fullness through Sexual Union

A complete six-CD program to learn the secrets to transforming lovemaking into a spiritual gift to yourself, your lover, and the world.

ISBN: 978-1-59179-083-9 / US $69.95

The Way of the Superior Man: The Teaching Sessions
Revolutionary Tools and Essential Exercises for Mastering the Challenges of Women, Work, and Sexual Desire

A spiritual guide for today's man in search of the secrets to success in career, purpose, and sexual intimacy—now available on four CDs in this original author expansion of and companion to the best-selling book.

ISBN: 978-1-59179-343-4 / US $29.95

For information about all of David Deida's books and audio, visit **deida.info**.

To place an order or to receive a free catalog of wisdom teachings for the inner life, visit **SoundsTrue.com**, call toll-free **800-333-9185**, or write:
The Sounds True Catalog, PO Box 8010, Boulder CO 80306.